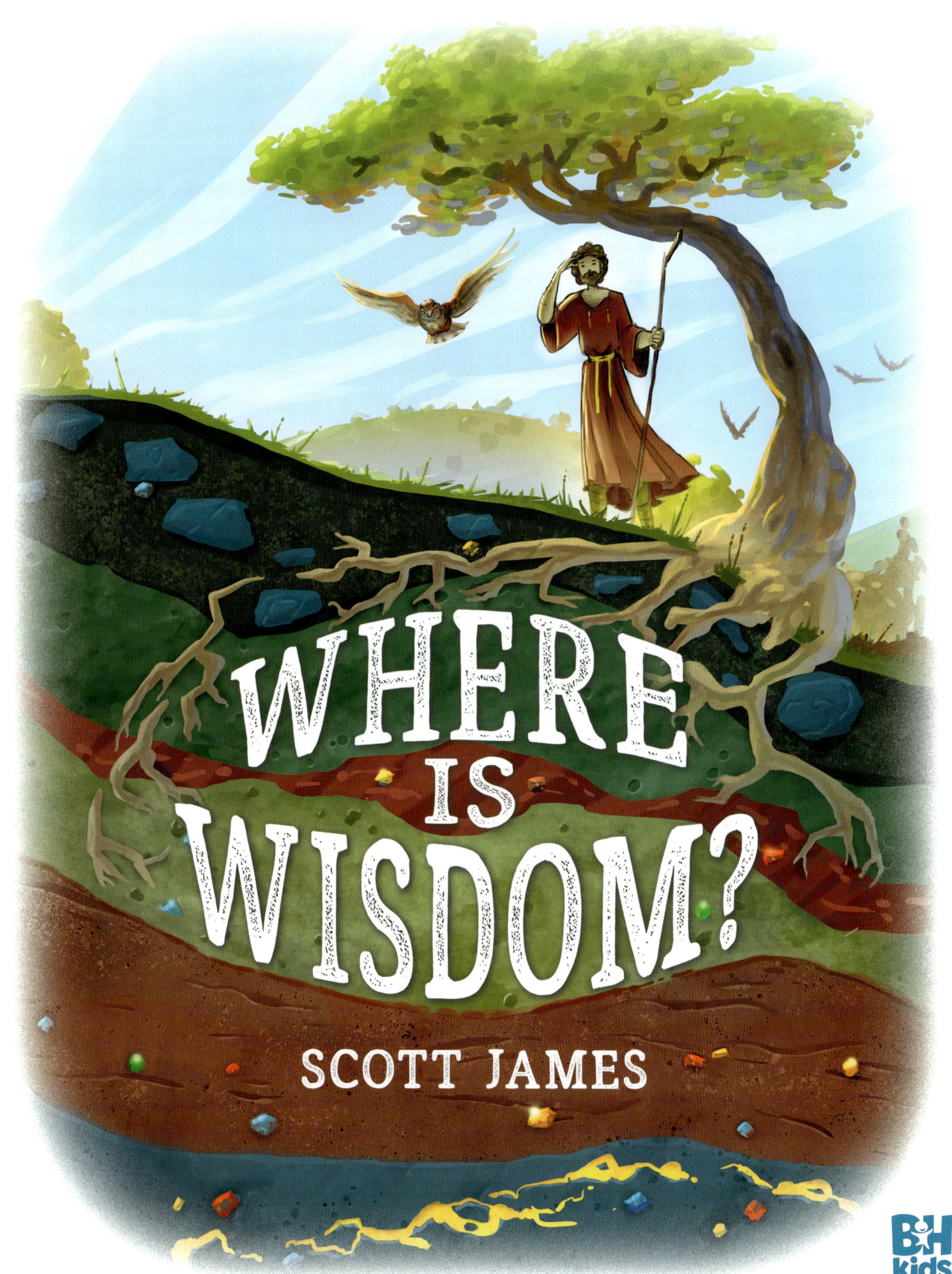

*For Kis, to point you to the One
in whom true wisdom is found.*

Copyright © 2020 by Scott James
All rights reserved.
978-1-5359-6596-5
Published by B&H Publishing Group, Nashville, Tennessee
Dewey Decimal Classification: C153.8
Subject Heading: BIBLE. O.T. JOB 28 / WISDOM / INTELLECT

Scripture quotations are taken from The Christian Standard Bible.
Copyright © 2017 by Holman Bible Publishers. Used by permission.
Christian Standard Bible®, and CSB® are federally registered
trademarks of Holman Bible Publishers, all rights reserved.

Printed in Shenzhen, Guangdong, China, November 2019

1 2 3 4 5 6 • 23 22 21 20 19

LOOK at this world the Lord has made! Beauty is all around.

God filled the world with wonders and sent us on a treasure hunt. Some treasures are easy to find. Others are buried away, hidden for those who seek.

The world is full of people who love to discover, to push back the darkness and find new things. They search far and wide to uncover treasure of every kind.

And how good they are at finding it!

Farmers work the dark soil and gather a prize of golden wheat. Miners dig deep to find troves of silver and gold.

There's treasure **EVERYWHERE.**

Burrowing beneath the mountains, explorers seek every precious thing—copper, iron, sapphires, and sparkling gems in every color. What priceless prizes the Lord has given!

In fields above, the beasts pass by without knowing what riches lie below. The lion prowls the earth and the hawk circles the sky, unaware of treasures buried deep.

So much remains HIDDEN to them.

The treasures of earth have been given to mankind, not to make us rich, but to show us how generous the Giver can be.

As good as these gifts are, God tells us to seek an even greater treasure . . .

WISDOM.

But where is wisdom found?
Where can we dig up understanding? Treasure hunters have searched high and low, but they do not know the way.

Some men try to buy wisdom with silver and gold, but it is far more valuable than that. Its price is greater than diamonds and pearls.

NOTHING compares to the worth of true wisdom.

WHERE, then, is wisdom found?

We hear whispers of it, but no one seems to know where it is.

Don't worry. Wisdom is hidden, but it is not lost. God alone knows the way; He knows exactly where wisdom is found.

HOW can God know?

God made all things and set them in their place.
He knows right where each treasure is found.
He sees everything under heaven and has never lost a thing.

And do you know what is even more amazing?
God doesn't just see all things—
He **RULES** *all things.*

To the wind He says, *"Blow **THAT** way."*
And the wind obeys!

To the sea He says, *"That's **FAR** enough."*
And the water laps right up to the shore!

If God can do all that, then He must be very wise! *He* can tell us where wisdom is found.

He created the map that leads the treasure hunter to the prize.

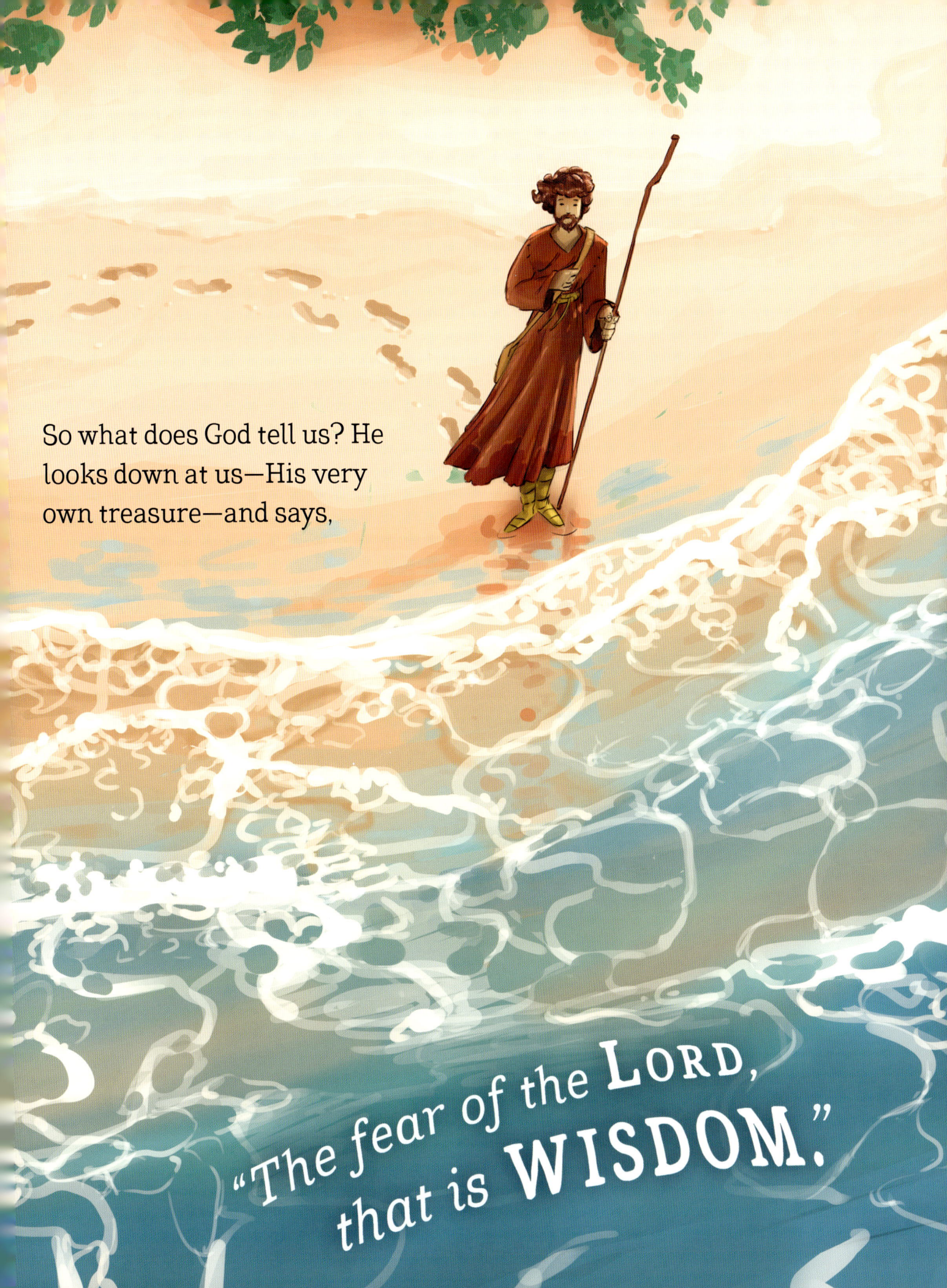

So what does God tell us? He looks down at us—His very own treasure—and says,

"The fear of the Lord, that is WISDOM."

The fear of the Lord—

to know God truly,

to be amazed by His greatness,

to want nothing more than to love and live for Him—

And now that we know of this generous Giver and the wisdom He provides, are we ready to see where this treasure hunt leads?

After searching high and low through God's wondrous world, we'll never find a greater treasure than Jesus Christ.

Wisdom points to **HIM.**

Remember

But God understands the way to wisdom, and he knows its location.... He said to mankind, "The fear of the Lord—that is wisdom. And to turn from evil is understanding."—Job 28:23, 28

Read

The Bible takes us on a tremendous treasure hunt in the book of Job, chapter 28. Take a few minutes to read this poem and look for any familiar scenes. You'll see people searching high and low, peering through the darkness and unearthing riches of every kind. But no matter how hard they look, true wisdom remains hidden to them. Job asks, "Where can wisdom be found?" (v. 12), and God speaks His answer at the end of the poem: "The fear of the Lord—that is wisdom." Now turn to Colossians 1:15–20 to read about our greatest treasure, Jesus Christ. God promises that whoever believes in Jesus will share "all the treasures of wisdom and knowledge" that are found in Him (Colossians 2:3). By trusting in Jesus, we can discover these riches today!

Think

1. This world is full of so many wonderful people, places, and things. What are some treasures you've discovered in your life? Who deserves the biggest thanks for these generous gifts?

2. As we walk through God's wondrous world in search of His treasures, we may stumble into some dark and scary places as well. Who can we turn to when we are afraid?

3. When telling us about the wind, the seas, the rain, and the lightning, Job gives us a picture of how God creates and controls the world. In Colossians 1, we learn that Jesus created all things and holds them together. Does that tell you anything about who Jesus is?

4. In this story, our treasure hunter ends up at the foot of the cross. That's an important thing about the fear of the Lord—it helps us understand we need a Savior. What gift does Jesus bring by the blood of His cross? (Hint: look again at Colossians 1:20.)

5. If we want to help others gain the treasure of true wisdom, Jesus is the most important person we can introduce them to. Who can you share Jesus with today?